IMAGES
of America

APPOMATTOX
COUNTY

ON THE COVER: Timothy O'Sullivan took this photograph of the Appomattox courthouse in the late summer or early fall of 1865. This is one of three photographs taken by O'Sullivan in front of the courthouse building. It shows Company D of the 188th Pennsylvania Infantry stationed in the village as the provost guard for Appomattox County. George Peers, the county clerk, is the gentleman standing atop the wooden stairs in the middle of the fence. With Peers are two children—most likely his—and another well-dressed Appomattox citizen. Capt. James Geiser is the officer standing at the left end of the Springfield rifle stacks; he later returned to Appomattox to fill the role of sheriff. A former Confederate soldier appears in front of the stairs still wearing his military uniform. At the top of the courthouse stairs, with his jacket open, stands Lt. Henry Cogan. Cogan married Emma Hix, the tavern owner's daughter. He later returned to Appomattox, became the postmaster, and is buried in the Hix family cemetery behind the tavern. The fourth soldier sitting on the fence to the left of the steps and the second soldier on the right are holding mascots, most likely dogs. The mascots moved during the photograph's long exposure, causing them to blur. Forty Federal soldiers appear in the photograph, as well as five civilians. Federal soldiers were stationed throughout Virginia as a provost guard—troops to maintain law and order until the reestablishment of government. In Appomattox County, portions of the 21st Pennsylvania Cavalry served as provost guards from May 15 to June 13, 1865. Then the 8th Pennsylvania Cavalry filled this role until July 22, 1865. Finally, Company D of the 188th Pennsylvania Infantry took up the provost duties until November 29, 1865. Capt. James Geiser, acting as the assistant provost marshal, set up his headquarters tent in the courthouse yard. The original courthouse was constructed from 1846 to 1847 and served as the county seat of Appomattox until it burned in February 1892. From 1963 to 1964, the courthouse was reconstructed for use as the park's visitor center. Neither Gen. Robert E. Lee nor Gen. Ulysses S. Grant entered the courthouse building at the time of the surrender. Since it was Palm Sunday, the courthouse was closed. (Courtesy of Appomattox Court House National Historical Park.)

IMAGES
of America

APPOMATTOX
COUNTY

Patrick A. Schroeder and Scott Frantel

ARCADIA
PUBLISHING

Published by Arcadia Publishing
Charleston, South Carolina

Library of Congress Catalog Card Number: 2008927827

For all general information contact Arcadia Publishing at:
Telephone 843-853-2070
Fax 843-853-0044
E-mail sales@arcadiapublishing.com
For customer service and orders:
Toll-Free 1-888-313-2665

Visit us on the Internet at www.arcadiapublishing.com

To the place where the nation reunited and its people
—Patrick A. Schroeder

In loving memory of my gentle and kind mother,
Charlotte "Sherry" Frantel
—Scott Frantel

CONTENTS

ACKNOWLEDGMENTS

The authors extend special thanks to: Watkins Abbitt Jr., Tom and Carolyn Austin, Virginia Babcock, Harriette Beasley, Helen Beaty, Mitch Bowman, Frank Brenner, Frank Brina, Bill Burke, Chris Calkins, James A. "Buddy" Connor, Betty G. Craft, Edwina and Julian Covington, Bill Cullen, Nancy and Raymond Dickerson, E. M. Drinkard, George Dodge, Zandra and Frank Elder, Butch Evans, Thomas Evans, Wanda Evans, John Fedison, Timothy Garrett, Angela Hamilton, Richard Hamilton, Marvin Hamlett, Cecil Harvey, Douglas Harvey, Paige T. Harvey, Sarah Horne, Beck Hudson, F. W. McFarlane Jr., Charles Meadows, Delbert Meadows, Becky Nix, Sheila Palamar, William Perrow, Kenneth Powell, Andrew Rakowski, Darlene Reed, Becky Rosser, Emily and Joe Sayers, Helen Scott, Chris Simpson, Donald Simpson, Kelly Smith, Ronnie Spiggle, Bobby Swanberg, Kyle Thompson, Clyde Trent, Lloyd and Shirley Walton, R. Gary Waugh Jr., Nancy Jamerson Weiland, Gerald Wilburn, Patsy and John Wilson, Barbara Williams, Joe Williams, Lisa Williams, and Frank Wooldridge; our sincere apologies and appreciation to anyone we unintentionally omitted.

Also, thanks to Appomattox Court House National Historical Park (ACHNHP), Appomattox County Historical Museum, Appomattox County Historical Society, Appomattox County Retired Teachers Association, Appomattox County Schools, Appomattox County Sheriff's Office, Appomattox Volunteer Fire Department, Appomattox Court House Presbyterian Church, Babcock House Bed and Breakfast, Carver-Price Legacy Museum, Circuit Court of Appomattox County, Clover Hill Village, Communication Design, Evergreen Baptist Church, Evergreen Presbyterian Church, Farmers Bank of Appomattox, Liberty Baptist Church, Library of Congress, Lynchburg Museum, Lynch's Landing, Memorial United Methodist Church–Appomattox, Museum of the Confederacy, National Archives, New Hope Baptist Church, Pamplin Pipe Factory, Alanson A. Randol (*Last Days of the Rebellion*), Rock Springs Baptist Church, St. Anne's Episcopal Church, Sons of Confederate Veterans–Appomattox Chapter, Spring Grove Farm Bed and Breakfast, Town of Appomattox Tourism Division, Tulane University, United Daughters of the Confederacy–Appomattox Chapter, Village Print Shop, Virginia Civil War Trails, Virginia Cooperative Extension of Appomattox County, Virginia Department of Conservation and Recreation, and Virginia Department of Historic Resources.

The authors extend our special gratitude to E. Wayne Phelps of Appomattox and our editor, Brooksi Hudson at Arcadia Publishing, for their enthusiasm and support.

A portion of the sales of this book will be donated to historic preservation efforts in Appomattox County.

INTRODUCTION

In the parlor of a brick house on a Sunday afternoon in April 1865, the course of the nation was set by two men: Gen. Robert E. Lee and Gen. Ulysses S. Grant. The path chosen was one of reconciliation and not of retribution. When General Lee addressed Lt. Col. Ely Parker of Grant's staff with the comment that it was "good to see one real American here today," the Seneca Indian chief responded, "We are all Americans." As Grant rode away from the McLean House and heard firing in celebration, he ordered the firing to cease, commenting that "the Rebels are our countrymen again." Lee, upon returning to his army, told his men to "go home and make as good citizens as you have soldiers." And the soldiers of the two armies left Appomattox, never to forget it. They left as Americans. Some returned in later years on pilgrimages retracing steps from their younger days, some from time to time in their memory. Some never left at all, making the supreme sacrifice in the final battles to remain buried on the field of honor. Over the years, millions of people have made their way to the tiny hamlet to experience the stillness of Appomattox and discover where the nation reunited. But there is more to Appomattox than the events of April 1865.

In 1845, Appomattox County was formed from the four surrounding counties of Prince Edward, Charlotte, Buckingham, and Campbell. The county was named for the Appomattox River, whose headwaters originate in its boundaries. The village of Clover Hill had sprung up in the center of the county after a stage stop was established at Alexander Patteson's Clover Hill Tavern in 1819, and with the formation of the county, it became the county seat and was renamed Appomattox Court House.

In Virginia, when "court house" is spelled in two words it signifies a town, the county seat. When "courthouse" is spelled as one word it indicates the physical building. This has led to much confusion over the years to many a student that learned that the surrender took place at Appomattox Court House, believing it to be a building, but it is actually a town, and the surrender took place at the home of village resident Wilmer McLean. This may be impossible to rid from the collective American understanding, but now you know and can spread the word. However, the rise of Appomattox Court House did not last long. Less than 10 years after the county was formed, the South Side Railroad laid track three miles from the village, and business gradually began to focus around Appomattox Station three miles to the west.

Prominent men rose in the county, and the tobacco business flourished with the growth of dark leaf tobacco. The labor-intensive crop caused the need for a large permanent work force, and prior to the surrender, nearly half the population of the county was slaves. With the election of Abraham Lincoln and the firing on Fort Sumter, Virginia seceded, and the troops raised in the county marched away to join the Confederate army. A half dozen companies were raised for service in the county, and most suffered heavily, but none more so than Company H of the 18th Virginia Infantry, commonly known as the "Appomattox Greys." They were at the forefront of Pickett's Charge at Gettysburg on July 3, 1863, and later sustained considerable casualties at White Oak Road and Sailor's Creek. Only one man was present with the company when it surrendered. Until April 8, 1865, neither army had entered Appomattox County, but the delusion of tranquility was abruptly shattered when Lee's Army of Northern Virginia came marching along the Richmond-Lynchburg Stage Road with more than 30,000 men looking to obtain supplies at Appomattox Station. The supply trains were there, but around 4:00 p.m., so was Federal cavalry under the command of 25-year-old Gen. George Armstrong Custer, whose men promptly captured the supplies and attacked the Confederate reserve artillery commanded by Gen. Reuben Lindsay Walker, leading to the Battle of Appomattox Station slightly northeast of the present-day town. Custer's men captured or scattered Walker's command, which had about 100 cannons. General Lee's line of retreat was blocked.

Lee held a council of war that night, and it was determined that an assault would be made in the morning to open the road and break out. The Battle of Appomattox Court House on April 9, 1865, ended with the withdrawal of Confederate forces from the west and Lee's army effectively surrounded just northeast of the village. The surrender meeting lasted an hour and a half, in which Lee received magnanimous terms from Grant for his men. The surrender ceremonies took place over the next three days, culminating in the stacking of arms of the Confederate infantry. Then the armies left, but some Federal soldiers returned to do provost guard duty in the county. Five of the Federal soldiers posted in Appomattox married local ladies, and two of them became residents of Appomattox Court House.

After the war, schools resumed and churches met, and except for the occasional curiosity seeker, life got back to what was deemed normal. Appomattox Station continued to grow. In 1892, the original courthouse burned, and the new one was constructed at Appomattox Station, also known as "Nebraska" or "West Appomattox." The McLean House was dismantled in 1893 to be reconstructed in Washington, D.C., as a Civil War museum, but it was never moved from the site. As Appomattox grew, the need for larger and better schools developed. The Appomattox Agricultural High School was established in 1909 and shortly after that a school for African Americans that was later given the name Carver-Price High School. Over the years, Appomattox has developed various businesses, favorite citizens, a few celebrities, a sense of community, and all around good people.

Appomattox's extraordinary date with destiny led to efforts in the 1930s to commemorate Civil War events and create a national park. The rebuilding of the McLean House drew national attention, and 20,000 people were on hand for the dedication. The crowds returned again on the 100th anniversary of the surrender for the opening of the new park visitor center in the reconstructed courthouse. Tourists from around the world still come to see the "surrender grounds." Each year its history draws more than 125,000 visitors to the area.

Today nearly 14,000 people reside in Appomattox County, but that number is only a modest increase since the county's formation in 1845. With government regulations, the tobacco culture has faded, and people have found other ways to make their livelihood. The people of Appomattox have created their own unique history with abundant churches, notable citizens, and special events that can be glimpsed through this assemblage of photographs. Though this is only a small collection of photographs used to illustrate national events and county history, much of which could not be covered, it is hoped that the reader will gain a better knowledge of Appomattox.

—Patrick A. Schroeder
Appomattox Court House National Park
Appomattox, Virginia

One

EARLY HISTORY

COUNTY FORMATION TO CIVIL WAR

Timothy O'Sullivan took this photograph of Appomattox Station in the late summer of 1865. On the evening of April 8, 1865, Gen. George Custer's Federal cavalry division captured the waiting Confederate supply trains here and continued to advance toward Appomattox Court House. The cavalrymen engaged Gen. Reuben Lindsay Walker's Confederate reserve artillery, captured 25 cannons, and secured 100 wagons along the Richmond-Lynchburg Stage Road. By 1865, Appomattox Station had become the county's center for business. Not only did goods arrive at this South Side Railroad stop, but so did the mail; a telegraph could also be accessed. In time, the community, known as Nebraska, that had grown around Appomattox Station became larger than the village of Appomattox Court House. After the war, another station was constructed, but it burned in 1923. A new station was constructed in the early 1930s that remained in operation for 30 years. Norfolk and Western deeded the inactive station to the town of Appomattox in 1973. The building presently houses the Appomattox County Chamber of Commerce and Visitor Information Center and the Arts and Crafts Center. (Courtesy of ACHNHP.)

Alexander Patteson built the Clover Hill Tavern in 1819 as a stop along the Richmond-Lynchburg Stage Road. It became the focus of the area, and the tiny village became known as Clover Hill. Later the village became Appomattox Court House. The tavern's kitchen, built about 1820, stands behind the main tavern building. It is the oldest structure that remains in the village. (Courtesy of ACHNHP.)

A group of Appomattox citizens posed in front of the Clover Hill Tavern for O'Sullivan in the summer of 1865, when Wilson Hix operated the tavern. Among the 20 civilians is county clerk George Peers at the center, with cane and children in hand. Several of the children are most likely his offspring. It was in the tavern that printing presses produced the parole passes for the Confederate soldiers. (Courtesy of ACHNHP.)

Samuel McDearmon (1816–1871) bought land, including the Clover Hill Tavern, in the new county seat of Appomattox Court House in August 1845. When the South Side Railroad passed west of Appomattox Court House in 1854, McDearmon sold his property in the village, reportedly hoping to move west to the Nebraska Territory. That dream never came to fruition, and the McDearmons took up residence in a house near Appomattox Station and dubbed it "Nebraska." (Courtesy of F. W. McFarlane Jr.)

In 1860, Wilson Hix, formerly of Diuguidsville (Bent Creek) along the James River in the northwestern part of the county, purchased the Clover Hill Tavern. Besides running the tavern, Hix also served at times as sheriff and deputy sheriff of the county. Hix owned the Clover Hill Tavern at the time of the surrender. Wilson Hix and several of his kin are buried behind the tavern in the Patteson-Hix family cemetery. (Courtesy of ACHNHP.)

Samuel McDearmon died in 1871, and the house was later sold to John R. Atwood, who did extensive remodeling. The front part of the house was added in the early 1890s. The McDearmon family occupied what is now the back section of the house. Current owners Capt. John and Patsy Guill Wilson have done extensive renovations to the Nebraska House, starting in 1993 when they purchased it, but the house retains its Victorian flavor. (Courtesy of John Wilson.)

Shown here is the Nebraska House as it appeared in the late 1890s. In the photograph are John Atwood (center), his wife, Florence (right), his four daughters Edith, Virginia, Jacqueline, and Lynolee, and his son, John, being held by a servant. Only three families have owned the house: the McDearmons, the Atwoods, and the Wilsons. Atwood was a former Confederate soldier who served in Company D, 19th Virginia Heavy Artillery. After the war, he became involved in the mercantile business and became one of the most successful and prominent men in the area. (Courtesy of John Wilson.)

Thomas Bocock (1815–1891) attended Hampden-Sydney College, passed the bar, and began serving as Appomattox County's first commonwealth attorney in 1845. Elected to the United States House of Representatives seven times, beginning in 1847, Bocock resigned in April 1861 when Virginia seceded. In February 1862, he was unanimously elected Speaker of the Confederate House of Representatives. A popular speaker, he developed a prosperous law practice and resided at the Bocock family home, Wildway, near Vera. (Courtesy of Circuit Court of Appomattox County.)

Joel Walker Sweeney (1812–1860) popularized a slave instrument called the banjar, today known as a banjo. Sweeney formed a group of traveling musicians called the Sweeney Minstrels. By 1840, he was a national celebrity, giving banjo performances throughout Virginia and in Charleston, Baltimore, Philadelphia, Providence, and New York. Sweeney and his cohorts became so popular in America that they toured Great Britain 1843–1845. He died from dropsy in 1860. (Courtesy of ACHNHP.)

Richard Alexander Sweeney joined his older brother, Joel, in the Sweeney Minstrels, but became ill while on tour in 1859 and died in Washington, D.C. (Courtesy of ACHNHP.)

Sampson D. Sweeney was the youngest of the musically talented Sweeneys. Not only was Sam an excellent "bangerman," he was a virtuoso on the violin. He joined Company H, 2nd Virginia Cavalry in January 1862 and was soon assigned to Gen. J. E. B. Stuart providing musical accompaniment. Sweeney died of smallpox at Orange Court House, Virginia, on January 13, 1864. (Courtesy of ACHNHP.)

With banjo in hand, Sampson D. Sweeney entertains at the headquarters of Confederate cavalry general J. E. B. Stuart. He is credited with creating the songs "Old Joe Hooker" and "Jine the Cavalry," among others. The rest of the Sweeney clan was musically talented as well, including sister Missouri and cousin Robert or "Bob," a left-handed fiddle player. (Courtesy of ACHNHP.)

The Charles Sweeney cabin still exists at Appomattox Court House National Historical Park. Reportedly, the house was used as the headquarters of Gen. Fitzhugh Lee the night of April 8, 1865. Charles, far left, served in Company H, 2nd Virginia Cavalry, commonly known as the "Appomattox Rangers," and later in Shoemaker's Company of Horse Artillery. His wife, Mattie Jane Bryant Sweeney, stands in front of the door. She was a noted seamstress, tailor, cook, and teacher. (Courtesy of ACHNHP.)

Joel Walker Flood Jr. became one of the wealthiest men in Appomattox County. He formed the "Appomattox Rangers"—Company H, 2nd Virginia Cavalry—in April 1861 and married Ella Faulkner in February 1862. After the Battle of Gettysburg, he joined the staff of Gen. James Kemper as a major and later was on staff duty for generals Longstreet and Pickett. Following the war, he served two terms in the U.S. Senate. (Courtesy of ACHNHP.)

Pleasant Retreat lies east of Rocky Run and before Vera, off present-day Route 24. At the time of the surrender, Gen. James Longstreet reportedly used this house as his headquarters. Pleasant Retreat was one of two estates owned by Joel Walker Flood Jr. (Courtesy of E. Wayne Phelps.)

The other Flood estate was Eldon, built around 1845 north of Appomattox on Route 26. This huge, three-story frame house with white columns was home to some of the area's most respected people, including Hal Flood; Eleanor Flood Byrd, mother of Sen. Harry Flood Byrd; and Judge Joel West Flood. The house remained in the Flood family until purchased by the Tylers in 1962. (Courtesy of E. Wayne Phelps.)

Henry Delaware "Hal" Flood was born at Eldon on September 2, 1865. He had a distinguished political record, first as the commonwealth's attorney for Appomattox, then as a representative of the Virginia State Legislature. While serving as a U.S. congressman in 1912, he introduced the legislation that made Arizona and New Mexico states and penned the bill that declared war against Germany in 1917. (Courtesy of E. Wayne Phelps.)

George Peers was one of the most respected and liked men of Appomattox. Before being elected the county clerk in 1860, he functioned as deputy sheriff and sheriff. He served as county clerk for 40 years, except for one term when George Abbitt held the office. Peers became known as the "Ambassador of Appomattox" and enjoyed regaling visitors with stories about the surrender and county history. He died in 1908. (Courtesy of the Museum of the Confederacy.)

The Peers House was built around 1850. D. A. Plunkett leased it to Peers, who purchased it in 1870. The last cannon shots of the war were fired by Confederate artillery posted in the yard on the morning of April 9, 1865. Lee and Grant met on horseback outside the house on April 10, and Gen. Joshua Chamberlain of the Federal army dined at the Peers House on the evening of April 11. (Courtesy of ACHNHP.)

George W. Abbitt, born in 1828, entered the Confederate service as a lieutenant in Company B, 46th Virginia Infantry, commonly known as the "Liberty Guards," and finished the war in command of the regiment. His sword is now on display at Appomattox Court House National Historical Park. After the war, he served as county commissioner of the revenue and one 6-year term as county clerk. Abbitt fathered 10 children. He died in 1878. (Courtesy of ACHNHP.)

Redfields was the home of George Abbitt and dates to 1830. On April 8, 1865, it lay in the path of Federal forces under the guidance of General Custer. Two wayward troopers entered the house searching for plunder, but Fannie Webb Abbitt, George's wife, ran out and appealed for help from a Federal officer. Unknowingly, she had called upon Custer, who entered the house and subdued the violators. Gen. Philip H. Sheridan used the house for his headquarters. (Courtesy of E. Wayne Phelps.)

Lewis Isbell, born in 1819, became the commonwealth attorney of Appomattox County in 1847. He was the local representative to the Secession Convention in April 1861. Isbell was a founder of the Appomattox Presbyterian Church in 1867. He became the first judge of the Appomattox County Court, serving from 1868 to 1872. He then moved to Chaiton County, Missouri, where he also served as a judge, and died in 1889. (Courtesy of Circuit Court of Appomattox County.)

Appomattox County sent four companies into Confederate service and supplied men to many other military organizations. The four principle companies raised in Appomattox were Company H, 2nd Virginia Cavalry, known as the "Appomattox Rangers"; Company H, 18th Virginia Infantry, known as the "Appomattox Greys"; Company B, 46th Virginia Infantry, known as the "Liberty Guards"; and Company A, 20th Virginia Heavy Artillery, known as the "Appomattox Invincibles." Here Sgt. Daniel W. Gills of the 2nd Virginia Cavalry strikes a Napoleonic pose. (Courtesy of ACHNHP.)

Two

THE CIVIL WAR YEARS
AND THE SURRENDER

Wilmer McLean and his family, who bought the Raine Tavern (built by John Raine in 1848) in the fall of 1862, were new residents to Appomattox Court House. McLean was from Alexandria and had married a widow, Virginia Beverly Hooe Mason, who had a plantation called Yorkshire (no longer in existence) near Manassas. Gen. P. G. T. Beauregard made his headquarters at the house during the 1861 Battle of Manassas, also known as Bull Run. (Courtesy of Patrick A. Schroeder.)

While in Appomattox, Wilmer McLean was involved in sugar speculation. General Lee's aide-de-camp, Lt. Col. Charles Marshall, was sent into the village to find a suitable place for the surrender meeting and encountered McLean. McLean offered a structure that was rejected by Marshall, as it had no furniture, before offering his own home. Here is one of only two portraits known of McLean. (Courtesy of ACHNHP.)

During the surrender meeting, the McLean family remained upstairs in the house. The family gathered on the porch in this fall 1865 photograph consisted of 50-year-old Wilmer; his wife, Virginia, who was 46 and expecting their daughter Virginia, who arrived on September 5, 1865; Wilmer's stepdaughters Maria (20) and Ocie (19); son Wilmer Jr. (11); and Wilmer's daughters Lula (8) and Nannie (2). Another stepdaughter, Sarah, had died in 1857. According to the 1860 census, the McLeans owned 18 slaves. The family moved from Appomattox Court House in 1867. (Courtesy of ACHNHP.)

The Battle of Appomattox Station occurred on April 8, 1865, when 25-year-old Bvt. Maj. Gen. George Armstrong Custer of the Federal army received orders from Gen. Philip Sheridan to advance on Appomattox Station and secure the supplies waiting for Lee's Army of Northern Virginia. Custer commanded a division of cavalry, some 3,000 men, and quickly captured the trains at the station. They then encountered the artillery of Gen. Reuben Lindsay Walker of the Confederate army and captured 25 of his cannons. (Courtesy of ACHNHP.)

The 2nd New York Cavalry led Custer's 3rd Division on April 8, 1865. This sketch shows members of the 2nd New York Cavalry capturing one of the trains at Appomattox Station. The supply trains had 120,000 rations to feed Lee's army. The trooper by the train, Pvt. Fred Blodgett, calls "hands up" to the engineer while leveling his weapon. (Courtesy of Alanson M. Randol's *Last Days of the Rebellion*.)

Gen. Reuben Walker, who commanded the Confederate reserve artillery, put his men into bivouac not far from the station along what is now Jamerson Lane. While his men prepared their food, Walker sat on a stump and was receiving a shave when Custer's column captured the trains at the station around 4:00 p.m. The battle that ensued proved disastrous to Walker's command and ultimately to Lee's army. (Courtesy of the Library of Congress.)

Pvt. Walter Jones of the 8th New York Cavalry had his life spared for the second time when the Bible he carried in the breast pocket of his coat stopped a bullet during the Battle of Appomattox Station, causing the hole in the center of the testament. The hole at the top came from a bullet at Cedar Creek. When the fighting stopped that night, it was clear Lee's army had been dealt a serious blow. (Courtesy of the Library of Congress.)

GEN. LEE'S LAST COUNCIL OF WAR.

General Lee held his last council of war at his headquarters the night of April 8. In attendance were generals John Gordon, James Longstreet, and Fitzhugh Lee, Gen. Robert E. Lee's nephew who commanded the cavalry of the Army of Northern Virginia. It was believed that only Federal cavalry blocked the Richmond-Lynchburg Stage Road to the west, and a dawn assault was ordered for the morning of April 9, 1865. (Courtesy of ACHNHP.)

General Gordon's infantry corps and General Lee's cavalry opened the Richmond-Lynchburg Stage Road to the west with an attack. After fighting through a cavalry screen, Gordon's men encountered Federal troops from the 5th, 24th, and 25th Corps. Gordon sent a message to Lee: "I have fought my corps to a frazzle." Gordon was selected by Lee as a surrender commissioner and led the stacking of arms ceremony. (Courtesy of ACHNHP.)

Federal troops from the Army of the James had marched more than 30 miles on April 8, 1865, to outflank Lee's army and again cut off their retreat. Gen. John Gibbon commanded the 24th Corps, which did the heaviest fighting on the morning of April 9, 1865. Gibbon served as one of the three surrender commissioners appointed by Grant and loaned his portable printing press to the paroling operation. Gibbon looked after the surrender proceedings after Grant left on April 10. (Courtesy of the National Archives.)

Lt. Charles Minnigerode was the favorite aide-de-camp of Gen. Fitzhugh Lee. He was severely wounded on the morning of April 9 when shot in the back, the bullet exiting from his chest. Exit wound blood and the hole from the bullet can be seen in the middle of his coat. Minnigerode's father received this note: "I am dying . . . our cause is defeated but I do not live to see the end of it." Left for dead, he was attended to by a Federal surgeon, and he survived. (Courtesy of the Museum of the Confederacy.)

A young boy stands in front of the Coleman House around 1930. The Coleman House area proved to be the epicenter of the fighting during the Battle of Appomattox Court House. Here the slave Hannah Reynolds was killed. A Federal field hospital was established behind the house. Near here, the 11th Maine Infantry received artillery fire and was attacked by cavalry. They lost 59 men, who were either killed, wounded, or captured. (Courtesy of ACHNHP.)

During the Battle of Appomattox Court House, a Confederate artillery shell passed through the house of Dr. Samuel Coleman. Though the Colemans had left the house the day before, their slave, Hannah Reynolds, remained behind and was mortally wounded when struck in the arm by a shell. Hannah Reynolds was the only civilian casualty at Appomattox. This photograph shows the path of the shell. (Courtesy of ACHNHP.)

Cpl. Hiram Williams, a member of the 198th Pennsylvania Infantry in Gen. Joshua Chamberlain's brigade, was struck by shell fragments when advancing on the village of Appomattox Court House and wounded in both feet. His left foot was amputated, as were the toes of his right foot, at a field hospital. Williams wore an artificial leg, or sometimes just a peg, after the war. (Courtesy of the National Archives.)

As Gen. George Custer's division moved northeast along the LeGrand Road, threatening the Confederate left flank, Capt. Robert M. Sims dashed from Confederate lines carrying a truce flag. Field artist Alfred R. Waud made this sketch of the occasion. This was the first truce flag, but not the only one; more than a dozen went out at various times in different portions of the line. (Courtesy of the Library of Congress.)

With his army surrounded, General Lee made arrangements to meet with General Grant. Around 10:00 a.m., Capt. Robert M. Sims (right) of Gen. James Longstreet's staff carried the initial truce flag, a "white crash towel" that he had recently bought in Richmond for $40 in Confederate money. A large portion of the towel is now on display in the visitor center of the Appomattox Court House National Historical Park. (Courtesy of ACHNHP.)

E. W. WHITAKER,
Captain, Co. E, First Connecticut Cavalry.
Highest rank attained: Bvt.-Brig.-Gen. U. S. V.
Born at Killingly, Conn., June 15, 1841.

With the arrival of Sims's flag of truce, Edward Whitaker of the 1st Connecticut Cavalry, senior officer on General Custer's staff, rode with Sims into the Confederate lines to demand an immediate and unconditional surrender, but General Longstreet would have none of it. Whitaker and Confederate captain John "Badger" Brown of General Gordon's staff then rode to stop the advance of General Chamberlain's brigade before more fighting took place, and Whitaker secured the towel as a souvenir. After the war, he received the Medal of Honor for gallant action at the Battle of Reams Station during the Seige of Petersburg. Whitaker is buried at Arlington National Cemetery. (Courtesy of George W. Dodge.)

The Widow Robertson House ("The Brick House") was built in 1842 and witnessed the last fighting on April 9, 1865. Confederate cavalrymen who escaped the noose encountered Union cavalry near this house, and a short engagement ensued. The Robertson family hid in the basement while bullets smacked against their house. The last Confederates to die in the fighting at Appomattox, Sgt. Robert W. Parker, 2nd Virginia Cavalry, and Cpl. William Price, 1st Maryland Cavalry C.S.A., died here. (Courtesy of ACHNHP.)

Lt. Col. Charles Marshall, Lee's aide-de-camp, was the only Confederate officer to attend the surrender meeting with General Lee. Marshall wrote Lee's acceptance letter of the surrender terms, and the next day, he penned General Order No. 9, Lee's famous farewell to the Army of Northern Virginia. Marshall was from Baltimore, Maryland. (Courtesy of Tulane University.)

Gen. Robert E. Lee, commander of the Army of Northern Virginia, met with General Grant in the parlor of the McLean House from 1:30 p.m. to 3:00 p.m. on April 9, 1865, which resulted in the surrender of his remaining army, some 28,231 men. Lee was 58 years old at the time. After a short time in Richmond, Lee became president of Washington College in Lexington, Virginia, and served until his death in 1870. (Courtesy of ACHNHP.)

Ulysses S. Grant was 42 when he met Lee at the McLean House. Grant commanded all the United States forces in the country. In the meeting with Lee, Grant offered very generous terms to establish grounds for reconciliation. Following the meeting, he left the McLean House and heard his troops firing their weapons in celebration. He ordered it stopped, saying, "The Rebels are our countrymen again." Grant later became president (1869–1877). (Courtesy of ACHNHP.)

Ely Parker was a Seneca Indian chief on General Grant's staff. Parker was said to have the best penmanship in the army and copied Grant's letter with the surrender terms for Lee. When Lee commented that it was good to see one real American at the meeting, Parker replied, "We are all Americans." Parker served as the commissioner of Indian Affairs when Grant was president. (Courtesy of the National Archives.)

Maj. Gen. Edward Ord of the Federal forces commanded the Army of the James at the time of the surrender and was present in the room during the surrender meeting at the McLean House. He poses here with his wife and daughter at the table that Lee used on the occasion. Ord paid McLean $40 in Federal money for the table. It is now in the Chicago Historical Society's collection. (Courtesy of the National Archives.)

Printing presses were set up in the Clover Hill Tavern to print out parole passes for Confederate soldiers to use on their return home. Gen. George Sharpe oversaw the process and made his headquarters here. The presses were kept running day and night until nearly 30,000 parole passes were printed for the Confederates. Printing presses can still be found in the tavern as they may have appeared in 1865. (Courtesy of ACHNHP.)

A graduate of Rutgers and Yale, George Sharpe had originally served as colonel of the 120th New York Infantry before taking charge of the Bureau of Military Information (a forerunner to the Secret Service), which was responsible for gathering intelligence on the Confederate forces for Federal general Joseph Hooker. By 1865, Sharpe was part of the army provost marshal's office, second only to Gen. Marsena Patrick. (Courtesy of Patrick A. Schroeder.)

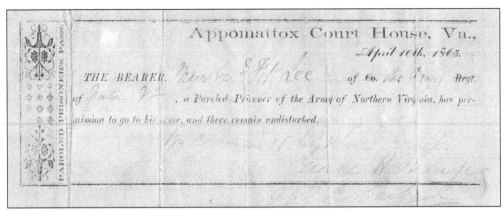

Parole passes such as this were given to Confederate soldiers to provide protection and help them to obtain services on their way home. The soldier could use the pass for transportation, food, and even clothing. A soldier's Appomattox parole pass became a treasured family heirloom. This is the parole pass that was issued to Fitzhugh Lee, and it was actually signed by Gen. George Sharpe. (Courtesy of ACHNHP.)

Lee and Grant met a second time at Appomattox. This meeting was on horseback near the George Peers house on April 10. Grant tried to persuade Lee to surrender the three remaining Confederate armies, as Lee had only surrendered the Army of Northern Virginia, but Lee declined. They also discussed the condition of the country. Lee and Grant met only one more time, in Washington, D.C., when Grant was president. (Courtesy of Charles Meadows.)

General Longstreet was General Lee's right-hand man. When Lee received a letter from Grant on April 7 asking for his surrender, Longstreet commented, "Not yet." Longstreet commanded the rear of the army at Appomattox and made his headquarters at Pleasant Retreat. Longstreet served as one of the surrender commissioners that met on April 10 to formulate the details of the surrender process. Longstreet had been a groomsman at Grant's wedding. (Courtesy of ACHNHP.)

Gen. Joshua Chamberlain's brigade led the advance of the 5th Corps on the morning of April 9, halting near the Mariah Wright House. Chamberlain's brigade consisted of the 185th New York Infantry and 198th Pennsylvania Infantry. On April 11, he was given command of his old brigade, which included the 20th Maine Infantry. A favorite of Gen. Charles Griffin, Chamberlain was given charge of receiving the Confederate infantry surrender on April 12. (Courtesy of ACHNHP.)

This illustration of the stacking of arms ceremony was produced by John R. Chapin, who received details of the scene from Chamberlain. The ceremony proved very emotional and touching. Chamberlain had his soldiers "shoulder arms" as the Confederates approached. This was a soldier's salute, to which the Confederates responded. More than 22,000 Confederate infantry stacked their arms on the stage road that day. (Courtesy of ACHNHP.)

Gen. John Gibbon assembled the men of his 24th Corps with flags captured from the Army of Northern Virginia in the Appomattox campaign for a ceremony at the war department on May 3, 1865. Gibbon stands in front of the tree. Even after Lee's surrender, three other Confederate armies remained in the field. Gen. Joseph Johnston surrendered on April 26, Gen. Richard Taylor on May 4, and Gen. Kirby Smith on June 2. (Courtesy of ACHNHP.)

Three

POST–CIVIL WAR AND THE CREATION OF A NATIONAL PARK

On April 16, 1950, more than 20,000 people gathered at Appomattox Court House for the McLean House dedication. Not only was Gov. John S. Battle on hand to address the crowd, but Douglas Southall Freeman, renowned historian and Lee biographer, participated as well. Though the rebuilt McLean House was finished in 1948, this was the official opening ceremony. (Courtesy of ACHNHP.)

The most famous painting of the surrender was completed by Louis Guillaume in 1874. Both Lee and Grant sat for Guillaume. Though the most famous, it has a number of inaccuracies, including Lee and Grant at the same table. Still, with the restoration of Appomattox Court House National Historical Park, local citizens contributed enough money to purchase the painting in 1954, and it now hangs in the park's visitor center. (Courtesy of ACHNHP.)

One of the inaccuracies in renderings of the surrender scene is the lack of correct people in the room. One person often left out is Robert Lincoln, son of Abraham Lincoln, who served as a captain on Grant's staff. Robert Lincoln (far right), an 1864 graduate of Harvard University, later served as secretary of war and was president of the Pullman Company, makers of the Pullman Sleeping Railroad Car. He is shown with, from left to right, Pres. William Taft and Pres. Warren Harding. (Courtesy of Library of Congress and George W. Dodge.)

George Frankenstein was a traveling artist who toured several battlefields in 1866 and made watercolor paintings to capture the landscape as it appeared during the war. He painted the features of the Gettysburg battlefield, and while visiting Appomattox, he made more than 20 paintings of its landscape, six of which are owned by the National Park Service and are on display in the visitor center. (Courtesy of ACHNHP.)

This Frankenstein painting looks into the village of Appomattox Court House from the west. The McLean House is on the right. The courthouse is to the far left. The white building closest to the road at center is the Old Raine Tavern, which was not in use at the time of the surrender, and beyond it on the right is the Pryor Wright House. (Courtesy of ACHNHP.)

The McLean House is draped in black on the occasion of the death of president and former general Ulysses S. Grant in 1885. County clerk George Peers, with the white beard, is seated on the steps. (Courtesy of ACHNHP.)

Shown here is a view of the Rosser shops on the right-hand side of the stage road. The courthouse can be seen in the distance. From behind the larger tree on the right, a Confederate soldier shot Lt. Col. Augustus Root of the 15th New York Cavalry as they charged into town on the night of April 8, 1865. The bullet passed through Root's neck, and he was buried nearby. (Courtesy of ACHNHP.)

In 1893, the McLean House was dismantled in preparation to be shipped to Washington, D.C., where it was to be rebuilt to house a Civil War museum. A panic in the stock market caused the Myron Dunlap firm to go bankrupt, and dismantled materials were left on-site. The materials rotted away or were taken as souvenirs. When the National Park Service reconstructed the house, 5,500 original bricks remained and were used in the reconstruction. A. H. Plecker of Lynchburg took this photograph of the rear of the McLean House, one of the last views ever captured, earlier in 1893. (Courtesy of ACHNHP.)

An 1892 view looks east of the area that was once called the "Surrender Triangle," though the name is a misnomer, as the Confederate arms were stacked all along the Richmond-Lynchburg Stage Road (to the left) from the McLean House to the Peers House on April 12, 1865. (Courtesy of ACHNHP.)

A. H. Plecker took this photograph in 1892 at the site where Lee and Grant met on April 10, looking east toward General Lee's headquarters. The Appomattox River valley had considerably less tree cover than it does today. (Courtesy of ACHNHP.)

Another 1892 photograph shows the area where Lee had his headquarters along the Richmond-Lynchburg Stage Road. (Courtesy of ACHNHP.)

The John Sears House is pictured as it appeared in 1911. The original house, which existed at the time of the surrender, is on the right. Family members gather in front of a later addition. The original house was reportedly used as headquarters for the Federal army's Gen. George Custer following the surrender. In the late 1990s, the house was struck by lighting, and both structures burned to the ground. (Courtesy of ACHNHP.)

Here is the west side of the Mariah Wright House as it appeared in 1922. Pictured from left to right are Anna Lee Godey, Myrtle Freeman, Larkin Freeman, Andrew Wingfield, Howard Freeman, and Robert Dunn. At the time of the Civil War, Mariah Wright was a widow. Her two sons joined the Confederate army; one survived the war, the other did not. Fountain Wright served with the 2nd Virginia Cavalry. Gilliam Wright enlisted in the 38th Battalion of Virginia Light Artillery and was mortally wounded at Petersburg in June 1864. (Courtesy of J. L. Freeman.)

These are the remains of the Appomattox Courthouse after the fire in 1892 photographed by A. H. Plecker of Lynchburg. After the courthouse burned, the seat of the county government was moved three miles west to the town of Appomattox Station, or what was being called West Appomattox, where a new courthouse building was erected. (Courtesy of the Museum of the Confederacy.)

This post-1906 photograph shows the new courthouse that was built after the old one burned in the village of Appomattox Court House in 1892. A new courthouse and county office building was built behind this structure and opened in 2005. This building is now used by the Appomattox Courthouse Theatre. (Courtesy of ACHNHP.)

Pictured here is the Confederate monument as it appeared in the early 1900s. The monument was dedicated on June 9, 1906. On October 15, 1954, the statue portion shattered as it tumbled to the ground when Hurricane Hazel passed through Appomattox. It was broken into more than 100 parts, and Sheriff David T. Robertson painstakingly pieced it back together; in 1957, it was returned to the top of the monument. The repaired statue was replaced in 2000 with a new replica through the efforts of the Appomattox Sons of Confederate Veterans, and the old statue is now on display with the historical society. Behind the monument is the jail, now the home of the Appomattox County Historical Museum. (Courtesy of ACHNHP.)

Here is a gathering of Confederate veterans by the Confederate monument around 1910. (Courtesy of the Appomattox County Historical Museum.)

Shown here are Stephen Thomas Marsh and his wife, Elvira Gordon. Marsh joined Company B, 18th Virginia Infantry, in February 1864. On April 6, 1865, at the Battle of Sailor's Creek near Farmville, General Pickett's division was virtually eliminated as a fighting force. The 18th Virginia was part of that command, but Private Marsh escaped by crawling through gullies and hiding in thickets. He reached his parents' home near Evergreen on the morning of April 9. (Courtesy of E. Wayne Phelps.)

Here a group of Appomattox Confederate veterans hold American flags around 1913. Seated at the far right, Daniel Ferguson holds his to the ground. He was shot in the face at Gettysburg. Pictured from left to right are (seated) Milton Isbell, George Cheatham, Mr. Grow, Robert Caldwell, Stephen Marsh and Ferguson; (standing) Samuel Ransom, Mr. Purdue, D. A. Christian, "Ove" Davis, Douglass Hancock, Charles Cardwell, and J. T. Campbell. (Courtesy of the Appomattox County Historical Society.)

In this *c.* 1932 photograph, Chauncey Comodore Ferguson sits on the runner of a car. Ferguson, born in 1837, served in the 46th Virginia Infantry. He was captured at Roanoke Island, North Carolina, on February 18, 1862, and paroled. Chauncey, better known as C. C., remained in service until April 1865 and then farmed in Appomattox, dying in 1936 at age 99. He fathered 25 children by two wives. (Courtesy of Tom and Carolyn Austin.)

A group of schoolchildren and their teacher rest on and peak in the McLean icehouse around 1915. The kitchen can be seen behind the icehouse. These structures were not dismantled when the house was taken apart. (Courtesy of ACHNHP.)

The group of schoolchildren then moved to the McLean House brick pile that sat waiting for a move that never took place. Curiosity seekers often took a brick home as a souvenir. More than 5,500 original bricks remained, however, when the house was reconstructed around 1948. They were used on the front portion of the rebuilt house between the windows and the front door. (Courtesy of ACHNHP.)

The school group moved to the old jail. This, in fact, was the second jail in Appomattox County; the original jail built across the road burned down prior to the surrender. This newer building may have used bricks from the old jail, as the brick color noticeably changes half way up the building. Recently discovered information indicates it was finished in 1867. It served as a polling station from 1892 to 1940. (Courtesy of ACHNHP.)

As provided by the act of 1930, a monument was to be erected by the U.S. War Department in the courthouse circle at old Appomattox Court House. This was the winning design for the proposed monument. The inscription in the peace memorial read, "North, South, Peace, Unity. Appomattox, the site of the termination of the War between the States." Strong local opposition to this monument prevailed, and a plan to restore the village was adopted. (Courtesy of ACHNHP.)

Three men gathered around the United Daughters of the Confederacy Monument in this view taken on April 23, 1942, of the courthouse area looking north toward the Clover Hill Tavern complex. A white sign points the direction to the National Park Service office. The monument was moved to the Confederate Cemetery when the courthouse was reconstructed in 1964. (Courtesy of ACHNHP.)

Here is another view toward the Clover Hill Tavern, this one taken by Fred Dudley of Lynchburg. To the right is a new sign that starts with "Appomattox Court House National Monument." (Courtesy of ACHNHP.)

This is the Meeks store as it appeared in the late 1930s. During the time of the Civil War, it was operated by Francis and Mariah Meeks. Their son, LaFayette, joined Company H, 2nd Virginia Cavalry, in April 1861 when he was 18 years old and died of typhoid fever at Manassas. His body was recovered and buried in the field behind the store. Starting in 1884, it served as a Presbyterian manse. (Courtesy of ACHNHP.)

In the late 1930s, African American workers of the Civilian Conservation Corps were posted in Appomattox and used for the development of the national park. Here Robert Scott supervises the men loading boards and other materials onto a truck. (Courtesy of Helen Scott.)

Here the Civilian Conservation Corps loads an uprooted tree onto a trailer. This could possibly be one of the trees moved to the McLean House yard to replicate trees that were there in Timothy O'Sullivan's 1865 photograph. (Courtesy of Helen Scott.)

Shown here are Robert Scott, who had been employed at Fredericksburg-Spotsylvania National Military Park before being posted to Appomattox, and other men working on restoring the Bocock-Isbell House sometime after 1939. (Courtesy of Helen Scott.)

The area where the McLean House once stood is surrounded by a fence, while a man examines some of the remaining bricks, possibly for reuse. The Meeks Store and the tavern guesthouse can be seen in the distance. (Courtesy of ACHNHP.)

With excavation of the McLean House under way, Nathaniel Ragland Featherston (left) shares his thoughts with archeologist Preston Holder (center) and park superintendent Hubert Gurney while Gurney's son sits at his feet. The photograph was taken on August 23, 1941. Much of the work at the park site halted during World War II. Featherston was born in the McLean House in 1874. The Raglands bought the house after the McLeans departed in 1867. (Courtesy of Helen Scott.)

After the McLean House dig, the next major area for excavation was the site of the courthouse building. Local residents assisted in the digging, sifting, and dirt removal. (Courtesy of ACHNHP.)

Workers make progress here in the McLean House reconstruction. (Courtesy of ACHNHP.)

Gov. John S. Battle addresses the crowd at the McLean House dedication on April 16, 1950. The feature speaker of the day was Pulitzer Prize–winning author and historian Dr. Douglas Southall Freeman. (Courtesy of ACHNHP.)

Present for the McLean House dedication were the progeny of General Lee and General Grant. Ulysses S. Grant III (left) and Robert E. Lee IV (right) cut the ribbon to the McLean House. (Courtesy of ACHNHP.)

The work went on to stabilize other buildings in the village. The tavern guesthouse is pictured here surrounded by lumber for support and scaffolding while men work on the roof. Originally built in 1820, the guesthouse is where travelers spending the night would lodge. Its unusual design makes the building a unique feature in the park. (Courtesy of ACHNHP.)

A young tourist reads the war department marker at the apple tree site. This is where General Lee waited to hear from General Grant in regard to the April 9 meeting. The legend about Lee surrendering under an apple tree started when Lt. Col. Orville Babcock and Lt. William Dunn of General Grant's staff met with Lee under the apple tree prior to the meeting at the McLean House. (Courtesy of ACHNHP.)

Memorial Bridge was built in 1930. It is 33 feet long and sits 11 feet above the Appomattox River. In the sides of the bridge are the Union shield and the Confederate battle flag. The bridge is on the National Register of Historic Places. Historically, this is the area where the ford for the river was located when using the Richmond-Lynchburg Stage Road. (Courtesy of ACHNHP.)

Looking east in this 1954 photograph, the large house to the left of the jail was called the Ferguson house. For a time, it served as a residence to park superintendent Hubert Gurney and foreman Robert Scott. It was later dismantled, as the building did not exist at the time of the surrender. The Peers house can also be seen in the distance. (Courtesy of ACHNHP.)

This is the view looking west along Route 24, which still passed through Appomattox Court House National Historical Park in this 1962 photograph. Only several locust trees appear where the original courthouse once stood. The Meeks Store and Woodson law office are on the left, and to the right is the stable, tavern guesthouse, and Clover Hill Tavern, at the time being used as the visitor center. (Courtesy of ACHNHP.)

The United Daughters of the Confederacy holds a ceremony annually on Memorial Day Sunday at Confederate Cemetery in Appomattox Court House National Historical Park. Pictured here is the program held on Sunday, June 1, 1958, where 19 young girls hold flags over the graves. The cemetery was established in the fall of 1866 and contains 18 Confederate graves and one for a Federal soldier, discovered after rest of the Federal dead were moved to Poplar Grove Cemetery in Petersburg in 1866–1867. (Courtesy of Carolyn Austin.)

In 1964, members of the Pure Company, dressed in 1914 clothing and driving a vintage car, stop in Appomattox Court House and shake hands with ranger Charles Meadows. On the 50-year anniversary of the company (1914–1964), the group was driving from Atlanta to Norfolk. (Courtesy of Charles Meadows.)

A throng of people gather in front of the newly reconstructed Courthouse Visitor Center during the events held on April 9, 1965, the centennial of the surrender. (Courtesy of ACHNHP.)

At the events held to commemorate the 100th anniversary of the surrender, Virginia Military Institute cadets fire a volley. Though the reconstructed courthouse building was finished in 1964 for use as the park visitor center, it was not officially dedicated until the April 9, 1965, event. (Courtesy of ACHNHP.)

On rare occasions, the Appomattox River has risen over its banks and flooded. For the most part, the Appomattox River is not very wide or deep, as its headwaters are in Appomattox County. (Courtesy of the *Times-Virginian*.)

A group of students who hiked the retreat route all the way from Petersburg to Appomattox Court House, more than 100 miles, poses on the steps of the McLean House with park rangers Chris Calkins (left) and Paul Ghioto around 1974. (Courtesy of the *Times-Virginian*.)

In 1974, horses were brought into the national park to add to the historic atmosphere, as well as to provide for mounted park rangers. Park maintenance staff members (from left to right) Louis Puckett, Roy Guthridge, and Henry Chernault unload Julianna (left) and Wakefield Denny (right) from the horse carrier. The horse program did not last long. After one of them kicked the superintendent's wife, Millie Lusk, and the perpetual care needed for the animals became clear, the program came to an end. (Courtesy of the *Times-Virginian*.)

The park staff gathers on the porch of the Clover Hill Tavern guesthouse in June 1977. Pictured from left to right are (first row) Ray Godsey, Frances Guill, Diana Purdue, Ava Almond, and Louis Garcia-Carbelo; (second row) David Spiggle, Johnny Carnifax, Harold Howard, Mel Dias, Henry Chernault, Helen Talbert, David Williamson, and Bill Talbert. Dias and Williamson were interns from Clemson University. (Courtesy of ACHNHP.)

Appomattox Court House National Historical Park was one of the first national parks to employ living history on a regular basis. Here the Widow Kelly (Ava Almond) chats with former Confederate soldier John Howard (Harold Howard). (Courtesy of ACHNHP.)

A Confederate soldier wanders along the Richmond-Lynchburg Stage Road west of the village of Appomattox Court House. In the background, the Clover Hill Tavern complex, snake rail fencing, and post and board fencing typical of the Civil War period can be seen. (Courtesy of ACHNHP.)

A young female ranger welcomes a park visitor with a brochure at the entrance station in the 1970s. (Courtesy of ACHNHP.)

Over the years, efforts were made to preserve the stately tulip poplar tree near the site of General Lee's headquarters while at Appomattox. At one point, when one side of the tree split open, it was filled with concrete, some of which can still be seen at the base. Ironically, all the efforts to preserve this tree were based on the belief that General Lee read his farewell address, General Order No. 9, to his men from under this tree, which never happened. Here in 1980, Supt. Luis E. Garcia-Curbelo and park technician Amy Ray look over plans for the beautification of the site, for which the park had received a $57,000 donation. The tree behind Garcia-Curbelo and Ray was grown from a sapling of the famous tree. (Courtesy of ACHNHP.)

Appomattox County resident and high school teacher Joe Servis explains the firing procedures for a Springfield rifled musket to a group of children at the park's annual day camp. The child closest to Joe Servis is Matthew Firth. (Courtesy of ACHNHP.)

Kyle Thompson of Fountain Valley, California, released an album called *From the Fields*, original songs of a Civil War genre that were recorded on battlefields across the country. Thompson was diagnosed with Lou Gerhig's disease in 2002. Given less than five years to live, he set out on a historical musical journey. Thompson is shown in front of the McLean house in 2004. Sales of the CD help battlefield preservation. Kyle Thompson is no longer able to perform, but the disease has not progressed as rapidly as expected. (Courtesy of Kyle Thompson.)

Four

SCHOOLS AND CHURCHES

Pictured here are ever-popular coach Gordon Bragg (wearing the hat) and the 1966 Appomattox High School varsity football team that went 10-0. This team outscored their opponents 336 to 26! Irie Mays rushed for 1,600 yards and scored 163 points, both record-breaking achievements. The high school retired his number: 32. Mays is second from left in the third row. (Courtesy of the *Traveler* yearbook.)

A teacher (either Mae Fannie Abbitt or Mary Frances Moss) stands in front of a log structure near the Oakville School. This single-room log structure served as the first school in Oakville starting around 1890. (Appomattox County Retired Teachers Association.)

Pictured here is the Oakville School around 1906. (Appomattox County Retired Teachers Association.)

Teachers Mae Fannie Abbitt, Mary Frances Moss, and Mattie Sue Moss (far right) gathered their students and a dog in front of the porch of the Oakville School for this c. 1906 photograph. Among the students are Earl Marsh, Mildred Harvey, F. M. Alec, John Moss, Guy Harris, Ethel Marsh Childres, and Ruth Marsh Williamon. The girl with the white bow in her hair is named Beth. (Courtesy of Appomattox County Retired Teachers Association.)

HIGH SCHOOL AND AUDITORIUM, PAMPLIN, VA.

Shown here are Pamplin High School and its auditorium, built in 1927. These buildings were used until 1956, when grades 8 through 12 were transferred to Appomattox High School. (Courtesy of Edwina and Julian Covington.)

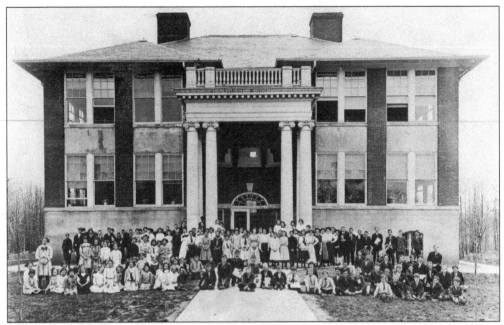

The Appomattox Agricultural School was built in 1909 and opened that same year. This photograph dates to around 1916. The first principal, Lindsay Crawley, served from 1908 to 1947. (Courtesy of the Appomattox County Historical Museum.)

Here is the Appomattox State Agricultural School Tennis Club in 1918. The members in the photograph are, from left to right, (first row) Viola Rollings, E. Kellogg Holland, and Kathleen Morgan; (second row) Harry Shotwell and George Martin; (third row) Ressa Evans, Robert Beale, Mortie Morgan, and John Zellers. Note the shadow of the camera and photographer on the ground to the right. (Courtesy of Appomattox County Schools.)

General Lee's soldiers stacked their rifles at Appomattox in 1865; the Appomattox State Agricultural School baseball team stacked their bats in 1920. (Courtesy of Appomattox County Schools.)

Is that a flock of Florence Nightingales? No, it's the 1920 Appomattox State Agricultural School Domestic Science Club, supervised by teacher Mary McConnell. (Courtesy of Appomattox County Schools.)

Pictured here is the 1921 Appomattox State Agricultural School Glee Club. Among its members are, from left to right, John C. Stanley, Harriett Clough, Dorothy Hundley, Marguerite Hancock, Carlton Crews, Sammie Ferguson, and John C. Caldwell. (Courtesy of Appomattox County Schools.)

The 1950 girls basketball team included, from left to right, (first row) Mary Ann Thompson, Helen Mae Poe, Barbara Carter, Barbara Ann Johnson (team captain), Beatrice Totty, Ann Goad, and Joice Christian; (second row) Virginia Chandler, Nina Barlow, Peggy Cole, Alice Hamilton, June Holt, and coach Louise Brown. (Courtesy of Appomattox County Schools.)

Pictured here is a typing class at Appomattox High School in 1950. How well would they do on a computer? (Courtesy of Appomattox County Schools.)

Fully uniformed, the 1960 Appomattox High School Band is ready to play. Pictured from left to right are (first row) T. Matthews, H. Pulliam, B. Williams, and B. Watson; (second row) C. Mays, S. Staten, C. Coleman, L. Harris, H. Harvey, B. Clapp, N. Burge, M. Barger, E. Ranson, C. Martin, J. Edmonds, and J. Sykes; (third row) R. Miller, J. Moon, T. Ashworth, E. Wilkins, C. Slayton, F. Wingfield, P. Thomas, D. Baldwin, D. Morris, R. Almond, and C. Richardson. (Courtesy of Appomattox County Schools.)

The 1964 junior class officers of Appomattox High School pose at the cannon by the river at Appomattox Court House National Historical Park. They are, from left to right, Vice Pres. Carrol Vandergrift, Pres. Joe Megginson, Secretary Barbara Staples, Treasurer Susan Burke, Reporter Judy Smith, and Historian Barbara Goin. (Courtesy of Appomattox County Schools.)

Shown here is the 1966 Robert E. Lee chapter of the Future Farmers of America. The officers in the first row include Advisor T. Johnson, Chaplain M. Torrence, Reporter N. Booth, Vice Pres. A. Carter, Secretary G. Chernault, Sentinel D. Torrence, and Advisor R. Carter. (Courtesy of Appomattox County Schools.)

The 1967 Junior 4-H is pictured here. The officers in the front row, pictured left to right, are Rep. Becky Harvey, Treasurer Plinky Williams, Secretary Jane Wagner, Vice Pres. Aileen Torrence, and Pres. Lucy Martin. (Courtesy of Appomattox County Schools.)

Shown here from left to right are Kathy Gunter, Cynthia Bryant, Kathy Jones, Alecia Moore, and Judy Bryant when they were members of the sociology club around Christmas 1975. Apparently, Judy Bryant was a fan of the movie *Jaws*, which was released the same year. (Courtesy of the *Times-Virginian*.)

Shown here are the 1960 Carver-Price District Girls Basketball Champions. From left to right are Roberta Ferguson Womack, Emma Hancock, Carol Andrews, Joan Turner McCoy, Beatrice P. James, Mildred Johnson Williams, Yvonne Johnson Bumpers, Kate James Walker, and Joanne Ferguson Randolph. Mozella Price became supervisor of African American schools in Appomattox County in 1919. Carver-Price High School took shape from 1926 to 1927 and was initially named for George Washington Carver. The original enrollment was 75 students. (Courtesy of the Carver-Price Legacy Museum.)

Carver-Price boys' basketball coach Joseph F. Lewis is pictured around 1969 with players Clarence Johns (left), Larry Robinson (center), and Leroy Wooldridge. (Courtesy of the Carver-Price Legacy Museum.)

74

Children are shown here in the classroom setting at Carver-Price School. In 1952, a new school building was completed and the name Carver-Price High School adopted. The building now houses the Carver-Price Legacy Museum. (Courtesy of the Carver-Price Legacy Museum.)

Students at Carver-Price are pictured around 1964 to 1967 enjoying recreational activities, including ping-pong and volleyball, as part of the May Day celebration that concluded by winding ribbons around a pole. (Courtesy of the Carver-Price Legacy Museum.)

This group photograph of the Teacher Aid Training Program was probably taken in the summer of 1966. Included are Betty Penn, Pamela Davis, Juanita Lawing, Ella Robinson, Eva Mac Johnson, Eva Allen, Ethel Poindexter, Grace Forrest, Edward Lockett, Cora Napier, Carrie Goode, unidentified, Delorec Hamlet, Evelyn Ferguson, and Mable Robinson. (Courtesy of the Carver-Price Legacy Museum.)

A gathering is pictured in front of Mozella Price's home, dubbed Camp Winonah. Students that did not have a family to stay with in Appomattox were allowed to reside with Mrs. Price at Camp Winonah. (Courtesy of the Carver-Price Legacy Museum.)

Rocks Baptist Church was founded in 1772 by Rev. Samuel Harris in a log building among the rocks along Swanee Creek. The creek offered a convenient spot for baptisms. In 1891, the church moved to a new site and built a new church on present-day Route 620. The church has expanded over the years and is now made of bricks. (Courtesy of Frank Elder.)

Rocks Baptist Church still conducts baptisms at Rock Springs. (Courtesy of Frank Elder.)

Evergreen Baptist Church formed with 89 charter members in 1907 and built this structure in 1908. The church was remodeled in 1954, adding a brick veneer. (Courtesy of Richard Hamilton.)

New Hope Baptist Church in Vera spawned from Wolf Creek Baptist Church. New Hope Church was built between 1831 and 1832. During 1853, the church counted 183 members, both black and white. It was in the vicinity of the church that Lee's army dug their last trenches and awaited an assault from the Army of the Potomac on the morning of April 9, 1865. After the war, the new church (the center portion shown here) was built. The side buildings were added in the mid-20th century. (Courtesy of E. M. Drinkard.)

The Presbyterian Church of Evergreen was originally built in Appomattox Court House in 1868. Founded by prominent citizens of Appomattox Court House, the Appomattox Court House Presbyterian Church congregation had been meeting at the Union Academy building starting in 1867. Rev. George W. Leyburn, previously a missionary to Greece, became the first pastor. In 1894, after the courthouse burned, the church was dismantled and reconstructed in Evergreen. (Courtesy of Richard Hamilton.)

With the demise of the village of Appomattox Court House, the Appomattox Court House Presbyterian Church was sold. The structure was moved piece by piece to Evergreen, where it was rebuilt by members of the Presbyterian Church of Evergreen. The Old Appomattox Court House Presbyterian Church built a new house of worship in the town of Appomattox in 1901. The congregation stands in front of that building on its 100th anniversary in 1967. (Courtesy of the Appomattox Court House Presbyterian Church.)

Memorial United Methodist Church formed in the new Appomattox Courthouse building in 1897. The church building in the photograph was built in 1899. The church has grown in size over the years and now is a brick structure. Here, Sunday school attendees assemble on October

Liberty Baptist Church started in 1834 when 11 members splintered from Rocks Baptist Church. This group also met in a log cabin called the Liberty Meeting House. A second building was constructed in 1855 and served as a hospital following the Battle of Appomattox. The patients

4, 1925, at the Methodist Episcopal Church South. In 1939, it became simply the Methodist Church. (Courtesy of Memorial United Methodist Church–Appomattox.)

who did not survive were buried outside. The last building was constructed in 1916. Here is the Liberty Baptist Church Sunday School on May 4, 1925. (Courtesy of Liberty Baptist Church.)

In May 1963, Liberty Baptist Church held a coronation service. The three girls at the top of the photograph—from left to right, Nancy McAden, Julia Ann Guill and Nancy Cole—received regent capes, the highest honors in the Girls Auxiliary. Jane Richardson and Lynda Hall received scepters. The theme of the service was "A Royal Diadem" in observance of the 50th anniversary of the Girls Auxiliary. Rev. O. Dalton Moore was the pastor. (Courtesy of Liberty Baptist Church.)

Elon Baptist Church in Pamplin was founded in 1859, and the same building is still used for services today. Interestingly enough, among the 19 founding members were some slaves. The first pastor was Elder J. S. Mason. (Courtesy of the Virginia Department of Historic Resources.)

St. Anne's Episcopal Church was founded by a small group of English immigrants who settled in the area of Spring Creek, now called Five Forks. This structure was built in 1875 and dedicated to Saint Anne, mother of the Virgin Mary. Over the years, the church fell into disuse, and in 1949, the property was claimed by the Diocese of Virginia. Hubert Gurney, superintendent at Appomattox Court House National Historical Park, became the warden of St. Anne's and had it dismantled and reconstructed in Appomattox, including 10 McLean House bricks placed in the cornerstone. (Courtesy of the Virginia Department of Historic Resources.)

This photograph is of animal celebration day where the animals are blessed in conjunction with the Feast of St. Francis each October. (Courtesy of Frank Brina.)

Mount Comfort was the three-storied home of Samuel Duval and, later, Col. John Johns, who called it "Mountain View." The house burned in December 1987 after being struck by lighting. (Courtesy of E. Wayne Phelps.)

Woodlawn Plantation, which dates to 1794, was a stop along the Richmond-Lynchburg Stage Road. In 1832, it was purchased by James Barbour, who served as governor of Virginia from 1812 to 1814, in the Virginia senate from 1815 to 1825, and as secretary of war to Pres. John Quincy Adams from 1825 to 1828. Confederate soldiers found bread and water awaiting them here on the way home from Lee's surrender. (Courtesy of the Virginia Department of Historic Resources.)

The Rock House at Eldon may date back to the Revolutionary War time period. (Courtesy of E. Wayne Phelps.)

The Williamson Home on Police Tower Road is shown here as it looked with snow on the ground around 1940. Parts of the house date to the 1800s, and the kitchen, which had originally been part of an old school house, no longer exists. (Courtesy of E. Wayne Phelps.)

This photograph of Rose Bower was taken in 1936. At the time of the Civil War, it was the W. J. Patterson Tavern. Lee's army and the Federal 2nd and 6th Corps all marched past this on April 8 and 9, 1865. The house is 2 miles northeast of New Hope Church along Route 24. (Courtesy of ACHNHP.)

A view of the Bocock-Isbell House shows children in the front yard. The house was built by Thomas and Henry Bocock in 1849–1850 and occupied by Lewis D. Isbell during the Civil War years. The building now serves as the National Park headquarters. (Courtesy of ACHNHP.)

Spring Grove Plantation was originally built by Dr. Reuben Palmer and his wife, Sarah E., in 1842. Palmer sold the house, originally comprised of 1,200 acres worked by 59 slaves, in 1861 to Baltimorean Joseph Wilson. It was bought by the Dyess family in 1908 and then the Beards in 1924. Spring Grove is now owned by Emily and Joseph Sayers, who restored and enlarged the home in the 1990s and now operate it as Spring Grove Farm Bed and Breakfast. (Courtesy of Joe and Emily Sayers.)

Annie Laurie Babcock is pictured here on the Babcock House porch in 1977. The front portion of this Federal-style house dates to 1884. Annie is dressed in Colonial attire in celebration of the bicentennial. She ran the cafeteria for the high school and primary school for more than 40 years. The Babcock House now serves as a bed and breakfast and has the tradition of serving some of the finest food in Appomattox. (Courtesy of Becky Rosser.)

Shown here is the Pryor Martin Cabin with Isbell Martin Grady at the front door in July 1981. This type of cabin was common to the area. Sturdily built, some still exist today. The Pryor Martin Cabin was dismantled in the mid-1990s and moved to Clover Hill Village. There were several cabins belonging to Pryor Martin and Pryor Martin Jr. in the area. (Courtesy of Frank Wooldridge.)

This is the first structure built at Clover Hill Village. The 6-acre village is run by the Appomattox Historical Society, which strives to protect early county architecture by moving buildings to Clover Hill Village, reassembling them, and restoring them. The present Clover Hill Village is a living history museum with restored or replicated historical buildings dating from 1820 to 1920. (Courtesy of James A. "Buddy" Conner.)

Five

FARMING AND BUSINESS

Edwina Miles Covington stands behind a stick of cut dark leaf tobacco on August 17, 1967. For 41 years, Mrs. Covington taught English, French, journalism, and media art in the Appomattox school system, including at the Carver-Price elementary and high schools. (Courtesy of Edwina and Julian Covington.)

This photograph taken of Billy Webber (1934–2008) in his Pamplin tobacco field in August 1960 will remind many of the long hours working the tobacco crop of Appomattox. (Courtesy of Kelly Webber Smith.)

Many a native of Appomattox will recall dark leaf tobacco fields like this one. In the early days of Appomattox County, dark leaf tobacco was a principle source of revenue in the county until government controls forced many of the small farmers out of business. Here some tobacco hangs after being "split." (Courtesy of Edwina and Julian Covington.)

90

On his farm near Evergreen, Fred Wooldridge rides on a grain binder as he drives three mules. The machine was used to bind oats, wheat, or other grains. (Courtesy of Richard Hamilton.)

Randall and Fred Wooldridge have a wagonload of hay ready to haul to the stable to feed the cows through winter. (Courtesy of Richard Hamilton.)

Local folks pitch in and load wheat onto a threshing machine on the Wooldridge farm near Evergreen. (Courtesy of Richard Hamilton.)

Therious Peter Robertson is pictured here on his tractor with Ellisen Scruggs. Born in 1870, Robertson ran a general store in Tower Hill but traded it to Roland Jamerson for a farm a mile north of Vera. His first wife, Roberta Megginson, died in 1916. The following year, Robertson married Irvin Coleman from Bent Creek, who was 26 years his junior. Robertson had two children by his first wife and four by his second. (Courtesy of Betty G. Craft.)

Taking a break from threshing wheat, ladies, children, and farmhands gather around the threshing machine on Therious Robertson's farm in 1925. When not farming, Robertson (standing at center with the umbrella) first attended Liberty Baptist Church before joining New Hope Baptist Church, where he became a deacon, though he did not like to pray in public. Robertson died in 1946 at nearly 76 years old. (Courtesy of Betty G. Craft.)

On February 20, 1965, in what's been referred to as "the great pig wreck," a truck carrying 159 pigs crashed at the intersection of Route 460 and Church Avenue. Nine of the hogs were crushed, but the other 150 escaped. By that afternoon, 75 to 80 hogs had been caught, but law enforcement officials speculated that several of the hogs might "unlawfully end up on some Appomattox dinner tables." (Courtesy of Donald D. Simpson.)

Harry Ferguson tends his garden. (Courtesy of the *Times-Virginian*.)

Customers and employees gather on the porch of the Appomattox Hotel for this photograph. The structure was built in the late 1800s by John Atwood, who moved to the Nebraska House in 1892. Thomas A. Smith and his wife, Nannie Legrand, ran the hotel until it burned down in 1917. (Courtesy of the Appomattox County Historical Museum.)

This *c.* 1915 view of the railway station at Appomattox looks toward the crossing of the Norfolk and Western Railroad tracks. In the distance are several automobiles, people resting under the shade of a tree, and the Bank of Appomattox on Main Street. Both the station and L. E. Smith's store attached to it (on extreme left) burned in 1923. (Courtesy of the Appomattox County Historical Museum.)

After the wooden station burned in 1923, Norfolk and Western built a new brick station in 1924. Passenger trains stopped running in 1971. Two years later, Norfolk and Western deeded the station to the town of Appomattox, which has used it as a visitor center and arts and crafts shop for more than 30 years. (Courtesy of the Appomattox County Historical Museum.)

Atwood Block on the east end of Main Street in Appomattox is pictured as it appeared in 1915. Located in the Atwood Building are the Charles F. James Drugstore and Brown and Smith's General Merchants. The Bank of Appomattox is on the left. Here two ladies pass in front of Brown and Smith's while William W. Burke crosses the road. (Courtesy of the Appomattox County Historical Museum.)

This 1915 photograph shows the view east to the end of Main Street at the Appomattox Hardware Company store displaying a sign that reads, "The Studebaker is sold here." A crowd waits outside the store for the results of a drawing. Behind the cars, carriages, horses, and people in the center is the Burke and Abbitt Insurance office, and on the right is the H. C. Babcock Company displaying a sign for shoes. (Courtesy of the Appomattox County Historical Museum.)

This photograph was taken around 1915 looking toward the east end of Main Street in Appomattox. People conduct their daily business here in town. On the left, a sign reads, "Peoples Drug Store." (Courtesy of the Appomattox County Historical Museum.)

In this unusual 1941 photograph of Main Street Appomattox, a cow is apparently ready to enter the Farmers National Bank. (Courtesy of ACHNHP.)

MAIN STREET AND N. & W. RY. STATION. PAMPLIN, VA.

Here is a view of Main Street Pamplin and another view of the station. This photograph shows a busy and prosperous Main Street Pamplin. Pamplin Depot was built in 1924. (Courtesy of Edwina and Julian Covington.)

This late 1930s photograph shows Rosser's Flour Mill just on the south side of the railroad tracks beyond Appomattox Station. Because of its location, the mill's products could be quickly and easily loaded onto the train cars, but its proximity to the track also resulted in it burning several times because of sparks. (Courtesy of Becky Rosser.)

Bandana Cabin Restaurant, located near the intersection of Pricilla Ann Lane and business Route 460, was a popular halfway meeting place for students from the all-female Sweet Briar and all-male Hampden-Sydney colleges. Run by Ada James and Mrs. D. N. Twyman, the restaurant is now only a memory preserved by Bandana Street. (Courtesy of the Appomattox County Historical Museum.)

This structure was built in the 1940s as a flour mill but was never used for that purpose. Instead, it was purchased for use by the Appomattox Garment Company. The Garment Company at one time employed several hundred people and produced up to 75,000 children's dresses a week, which were easily shipped out by train from Appomattox Station. Presently, Country Charm gift shop occupies this building. (Courtesy of the Virginia Department of Historic Resources.)

This 1952 photograph shows postmaster J. K. Hamilton waiting for the next mail train. With him are several cartloads of packages from the Appomattox Garment Company to be shipped at Evergreen. Business was so brisk for the garment company that several warehouses were used for storage, including one in Evergreen. (Courtesy of Richard Hamilton.)

Postmaster J. K. Hamilton stands atop a mail crane to which he attached the last mail bag to be picked up by train at Evergreen on December 4, 1965. (Courtesy of Richard Hamilton.)

If one were feeling ill in 1921, one could call on Charles F. "Charlie" James, apparently otherwise known as "Dr. Good," where he sold "Drugs and Other Things Where Lee Surrendered." He would have been useful for the ill soldiers that were at Appomattox in 1865. (Courtesy of Appomattox County Schools.)

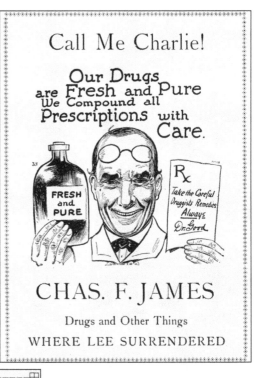

Call Me Charlie!

Our Drugs
are Fresh and Pure
We Compound all
Prescriptions with
Care.

FRESH
and
PURE

Rx
Take the Careful
Druggists Remedies
Always
Dr. Good

CHAS. F. JAMES

Drugs and Other Things

WHERE LEE SURRENDERED

H. D. FLOOD, President   R. F. BURKE, Vice-President   R. L. BURKE, Cashier

The Bank of Appomattox
APPOMATTOX :: VIRGINIA

CAPITAL, $20,000.00 - - SURPLUS and PROFITS, $30,000.00
TOTAL RESOURCES OVER, $365,000.00

A "Roll of Honor Bank"

Is one possessing surplus and profits in excess of capital, thus giving tangible evidence of strength and security. Of the 29,000 banks in the United States, only one in ten occupies this proud position.

We are among the number.

Nineteen years of progressive growth without a loss is conclusive evidence that this is a safe place to deposit your money.

Open an account with us, and we guarantee satisfaction. One dollar will start an account with us.

Our Officers and Directors are men of experience and ability who will always extend any and every service consistant with sound banking methods.

4% PAID ON TIME DEPOSITS

DIRECTORS:

H. D. FLOOD   JOS. BUTTON   C. F. JAMES   I. E. SMITH   C. W. SMITH
J. E. SEARS   S. L. FERGUSON   R. F. BURKE   R. L. BURKE

"THE OLDEST AND LARGEST BANK IN APPOMATTOX COUNTY"

This 1920 advertisement boasts that the Bank of Appomattox, located on Main Street, had over $365,000 in total resources. A surplus and profit exceeding the capital had the Bank of Appomattox listed as a "Roll of Honor Bank." Only 10 percent of the 29,000 banks in the United States attained that status. (Courtesy of Appomattox County Schools.)

Established on Main Street in 1918 with $50,000 in capital and C. W. Hancock as president, Farmers National Bank has always been there for the people of Appomattox. By 1960, the bank had outgrown its original facilities and had to temporarily move operations into the hardware store (seen here) while remodeling took place. The bank staff made the best of it and was quickly serving customers again. (Courtesy of Thomas Evans.)

On October 23, 1961, Farmers National Bank reopened its office in modern facilities on Main Street. In September 1973, a branch office was opened at Triangle Shopping Center. The downtown office expanded again in 1975, creating additional office space. Today the "hometown bank" continues to serve "hometown folks." (Courtesy of Thomas Evans.)

Pamplin Smoking Pipe Manufacturing Company, Inc., began making clay pipes in 1878. It was the largest factory of its kind and could produce 25,000 pipes a day. (Courtesy of Nancy and Raymond Dickerson.)

A local favorite, Maude's Restaurant was nationally famous for Southern cooking. It was located a mile west of Appomattox along Route 460. Maude Goff opened her restaurant in 1946 just east of Appomattox, but the business later moved west of town. There are a couple of spaces open for the next hungry customer at Maude's Restaurant, as it appears here in 1976. (Courtesy of the *Times-Virginian*.)

Pictured on the steps of the *Times-Virginian* newspaper office are, from left to right, (first row) state senator Howard P. Anderson and Watkins M. Abbitt; (second row) Harry Gordon Lawson and J. Franklin Vaughn. This local newspaper was founded in 1892. (Courtesy of the *Times-Virginian*.)

Bobbie Osborne (left) and customer Tammy Carter hold a five-foot sub at the Caboose Sub Shop in 1985. A local favorite, the Caboose Sub Shop operated in Appomattox from 1983 to 2003. (Courtesy of the *Times-Virginian*.)

Six

PEOPLE, ORGANIZATIONS, EVENTS, AND RECREATION

Shown here in 1967 is a scene from Spencer's Drug Store. While most people sip on sodas or malts, the young man in the center looks like he's getting ready to eat a knuckle sandwich. This place was a favorite hangout, especially after football games. It is now the site of the Village Print Shop. (Courtesy of Appomattox County Schools.)

George Austin operated a blacksmith shop in Appomattox. This photograph was taken of him with a hammer and anvil about 1900. (Courtesy of the Appomattox County Historical Museum.)

Irvin Dewitt Coleman (third from the back) is among those in the horse-drawn wagon at Bent Creek on January 2, 1908. Note the mud-slathered wheels. (Courtesy of Betty G. Craft.)

Pictured in 1910, Mary Catherine "Kate" Coleman (left) and Irvin Dewitt Coleman (right) are ready to travel sidesaddle on mule. Their friend Vincent Thornhill keeps the mule from moving for the photograph. (Courtesy of Betty G. Craft.)

On their way to somewhere in Appomattox are, from left to right, (back seat) Verta Smith Stanley, Ruby Walton, (front seat) Caille Babcock, and Rachel Ferguson Lawson in a surrey pulled by a pony named Billy Boy around 1914. (Courtesy of the Appomattox County Historical Museum.)

"Where did you get that hat" is written on the back of this photograph of Mary Virginia Godwin and her beau. Mary later said her vows to another man, Charles T. Moses Sr. The high-spirited lass was born in 1886 and died in 1964. (Courtesy of Virginia Babcock.)

This is the Chancey Comodore Ferguson family around 1912. From left to right are (first row) Hattie, Minnie, Nannie holding Hallie, Hop, Evans, and Dewey; (second row) Esther, Nettie, Bertha, Alice, and family friend Georgia Williams. Nannie Harris Ferguson was Chancey's second wife. His first wife was Emmaline Sydney Ferguson. Together, they bore Chancey 25 children. (Courtesy of Carolyn and Tom Austin.)

This late 1941 photograph is believed to have been taken in front of Charmos, formerly the Clem Hancock house on Lee Grant Avenue. Pictured from left to right are Charles T. Moses, Mary Virginia Godwin Moses, Webb Babcock Jr., Virginia Moses Babcock, Clara Matilda Mann Moses, and Thomas Walker "Tam" Moses. Charles T. Moses served as a Democratic state senator for Appomattox, Buckingham, Charlotte, and Cumberland Counties from 1934 until his death in 1964. (Courtesy of Virginia Babcock)

Le Roy Williamson (left) and his cousin Mervyn "Skippy" Williamson Jr. (right) don sailor's caps and play with a homemade baseball bat in this photograph from 1945. (Courtesy of E. Wayne Phelps.)

The family farm of W. L. Williamson is shown here around 1945. In the foreground from left to right are Bill Williamson, Audrey Williamson Phelps, Nell Williamson Cabaniss, Rhoda Williamson, Melva Williamson, and Ruby Williamson. W. L. Williamson is in the background on top of a cart loaded with hay, ready to put it in the old barn. (Courtesy of E. Wayne Phelps.)

The Howard Wesley Phelps family is pictured at the Phelps home in Oakville on a Sunday afternoon in 1946. From left to right are (first row) Edmonia Boyer and son David, Pauline Phelps, Doris Evans, Howard Phelps and Le Roy Chidester; (second row) Reginald and Eleanor Phelps, Odelta Evans, Ruby and Lenwood Phelps and their baby boy Ray, and Everette and Audrey Phelps and their son Everrette Wayne. (Courtesy of E. Wayne Phelps.)

Ready for an old-fashioned western shoot out, E. Wayne Phelps scurried atop of his father's Farmall Cub Tractor around 1949. The tractor is still in use. Wayne's father purchased the tractor in 1949 for $850. The tractor was sold shortly thereafter to make payment on a farm. In 1997, Wayne reacquired the tractor and restored it. (Courtesy of E. Wayne Phelps.)

Richard Simpson (1941–2006) is pictured in his state police uniform in May 1963. Fresh out of the State Police Academy in 1963, Simpson was posted to Wise County before being stationed in Appomattox in 1964. (Courtesy of Donald D. Simpson.)

Appomattox native Larry Robinson attended Carver-Price High School from 1965 to 1969 and was senior class president. Later he was part of the University of Tennessee's 1972 championship basketball team. He went on to play professional football for the Dallas Cowboys as a running back in 1973. (Courtesy of the *Times-Virginian*.)

In 1975, the Macmillan Publishing Company released Appomattox resident Traphes Bryant's *Dog Days at the White House: From Truman to Nixon, the Outrageous Memoirs of the Presidential Kennel Keeper.* In an anecdote from the book, Bryant quotes a supervisor who advised a complaining staffer bitten by Kennedy's Welsh terrier, Charlie, to "leave it be. If it came to a choice of who would have to go, you would be packing to leave, not Charlie." (Courtesy of the *Times-Virginian*.)

Tobacco work ran in the Webber family. Here 16-year-old Kelly Webber, who spent many an hour in her father's tobacco field, is pictured at the Virginia Dark Fired Tobacco Growers Market Association 4-H Tobacco Growers Contest. Webber received an award in the form of a $100 check as the top winner in the western district for 1985–1986 for the detailed records she kept during her preparations for marketing the tobacco crop. (Courtesy of the *Times-Virginian*.)

Charles T. Moses Jr. attended the Virginia Military Institute and studied engineering. In World War II, he was a first lieutenant in the Corps of Engineers in both the European and Pacific theaters. He served on the Appomattox Town Council and as mayor of Appomattox, as well as commander of American Legion Post No. 104. He was also the president and owner of Moses Motor Company. (Courtesy of Virginia Babcock.)

Watkins M. Abbitt Sr. (left) presents a donation to Charles T. Moses Jr. (right) around 1980 in front of the eternal flame. Moses, born August 13, 1922, was the founder of the Appomattox Eternal Flame, which was erected in May 1971 to honor the Appomattox war dead. Moses died on January 9, 2002. "Watt" Abbitt was a lawyer, commonwealth attorney, and congressman. Both men were well loved by the Appomattox community. (Courtesy of the *Times-Virginian*.)

Pictured is American Legion Post No. 104 in the late 1990s. From left to right are (seated) Charles T. Moses, Ivey Holland, and Buster Lucado; (second row) Keith Hamilton, Gilbert Mays, Albert Fratic, Butch Evans, Newton Jennings, and John McDermott; (third row) J. D. Martin, Cliford Harvey, Jesse Osborne, John Seaquist, Hunt Hamilton, and unidentified. The post was chartered on March 31, 1937, with 30 members. (Courtesy of E. Wayne Phelps.)

Shown here is Julius Williams, who received the Presidential Academic Fitness Award for outstanding academic achievement. (Courtesy of the *Times-Virginian*.)

Local farmers are pictured on a controlled burn in 1989. From left to right are Willis Carter, Leonard Garrett, Berkley Garrett, and Nathan Garrett. The Garretts were brothers. Leonard Garrett spent many a day on lookout in the Piney Mountain fire tower. (Courtesy of Betty G. Craft.)

Before this fire truck was ordered in 1946, the Appomattox Volunteer Fire Company hauled their water supply on the back of a Model T that sometimes had to be push-started. This was the first modern pumper for the station and it towed a hose cart. This truck did such good service that it was used to fight fires until 1986. The fire department still brings it out on special occasions. (Courtesy of Frank Brenner.)

Shown here is a Farmers Bank shareholders' dinner on January 8, 1952. Beverly Martin and Ellen Martin are in the bottom right corner of the photograph. Ellen Martin (right) worked for Farmers Bank, and Beverly Martin (second from right), a local farmer, was a shareholder. For years, Beverly brought in a supply of eggs weekly from his farm to distribute among bank employees. (Courtesy of Thomas Evans.)

In November 1953, Farmers Bank initiated a children's savings program using the popularity of Hopalong Cassidy. To promote the program, bank staff and many of the children dressed as cowboys or cowgirls. Though Hopalong Cassidy began as a book character in 1906, he was later developed into a radio, television, and comic book character. Marshall Goin is the boy in the center of the photograph, while John Evans stands under the Hopalong Cassidy sign wearing the cowboy hat. Bill Burke is to the right of lady in front of the window, and Sandra Robertson is in the center of the photograph, the third person back in the middle. (Courtesy of Thomas Evans.)

Paul Drinkard acting as Hopalong Cassidy assists a young girl, while Watkins Abbitt Jr. stands to the left between Jessalyn Drinkard (far left) and Eleanor Conner. Dewitt Evans is the man in the middle with his right arms stretched out, and Ethel Evans is in cowgirl attire under the Hopalong Cassidy sign. The popularity of Hopalong Cassidy exploded when, in 1949, it became the first network television Western series, and a huge merchandising boom also developed. Cassidy was a good cowboy who wore black. (Courtesy of Thomas Evans.)

After traffic deaths in Appomattox County jumped from one in 1954 to six in 1955, the Appomattox County Home Demonstration Club started "an all out traffic safety education drive" in 1956. The club's creed was "as homemakers, we will strive to have our organization foster the highest ideals in our homes and in our communities." Representing the club are Evelyn S. Hubbard (left) and Lola Morris. (Courtesy of the Virginia Cooperative Extension Office–Appomattox.)

The Home Demonstration Club noted that "traffic safety [is] one of our highest ideals." The club held a poster contest and arranged with the State Department of Education and the Virginia State Police to bring in their safety demonstration car for a program on April 4, 1956. A large crowd gathered for the reaction and braking test program on Highland Avenue in which town police officer E. T. Mitchell participated. (Courtesy of the Virginia Cooperative Extension Office–Appomattox.)

The Home Demonstration Club entered a traffic safety float in the Appomattox County parade on April 21, 1956, in the form of a towed, wrecked car with a banner that read, "Don't let this happen to you!" A man on horseback followed the car with a sign that read, "Slow but Sure." (Courtesy of the Virginia Cooperative Extension Office–Appomattox.)

On March 30, 1956, Elizabeth Carr (center) and Louise Martin (not shown) of the Appomattox Home Demonstration Club appeared on WLVA-TV, Lynchburg, Channel 13 at 7:00 p.m. for a program on traffic safety. Also appearing were Capt. W. W. Blythe (left) and Mrs. Goode Robinson (right). Mrs. Carr discussed efforts to promote traffic safety. (Courtesy of the Virginia Cooperative Extension Office–Appomattox.)

In 1973, the Appomattox Junior Women's Club inducted these officers. From left to right are Ann Ferguson, Nancy Elder, Judy Deavers, Becky Carter, Frances Guill, Edith Scruggs, and Lucy Woodall Harris, who was present for the installation of the officers. (Courtesy of the *Times-Virginian*.)

Members of the Lions Club gather to sell brooms in 1974. From left to right are John McLean, John Grinels, John Cole, Francis Elliott, Lloyd Walton, Rev. Cecil Dalton, and Dewitt Evans. (Courtesy of the *Times-Virginian*.)

Mayor Ronnie Spiggle signs a proclamation in 1990 for the Future Business Leaders of America, who have all donned their "I love Appomattox" pins. The students with visible faces are, from left to right, Cheri Chamberlain, Mary Kennedy, Melissa Bryant, Jackie King, Mary Helen McLaughlin, Heather Bryan, Nakina Gimbert, Jennifer Alvis, and an unidentified German exchange student. Spiggle served as the mayor of Appomattox from 1978 to 2006, the longest term in the history of Appomattox. (Courtesy of the *Times-Virginian*.)

For the 100th anniversary of the founding of Appomattox County, Senator and former governor (1926–1930) Harry Flood Byrd gave an address from the porch of the courthouse building. From left to right behind Governor Byrd are Rev. W. M. Black, C. W. Smith, Nathaniel Ragland Featherston, Sen. Robert Russell and professor John G. Fisher. Byrd had ties to the Flood family of Appomattox. (Courtesy of the Appomattox County Historical Museum.)

On April 7, 1949, a delegation presented Pres. Harry S. Truman with a plate featuring the McLean House. From left to right, the group from Appomattox consisted of Leonard Anderson, J. C. Hudgins, Watkins M. Abbitt, David T. Robertson, C. H. Robinson, J. H. Lucado, and unidentified. Truman himself was a Civil War enthusiast and had ancestors that served in the Confederate army. He toured Lee's retreat route in 1941. (Courtesy of the Appomattox County Historical Museum.)

On October 10, 1961, a family and their dog stopped in Appomattox on their journey from Providence Forge, Virginia, to California. Drawn by two mules, their conveyance was dubbed "The Last Wagon West." (Courtesy of the Appomattox County Historical Museum.)

Music plays at the first Historic Appomattox Railroad Festival in 1972. Pictured from left to right are Sam Conner, Bill Williamson, Tom Childress, Ruth "Betty" Scruggs, and Judge George F. Abbitt. The festival has been an annual event ever since, now drawing more than 35,000 people to the parade, crafts, food, and music. (Courtesy of Kenneth Powell.)

Appomattox Middle School students dress in anticipation of the Historic Appomattox Railroad Festival in 1974. Each student dressed for school in historical garb, lending to the spirit of the occasion. There appears to be a Johnny Appleseed among the lot. (Courtesy of the *Times-Virginian*.)

A future fireman rides in the parade at the annual Historic Appomattox Railroad Festival, held every October. (Courtesy of the *Times-Virginian*.)

The annual James River Bateau Festival passes through Appomattox. Historically, bateaux were used on the James River to haul tobacco or other cargo to market from 1775 to 1840. They were replaced by packet boats soon after. The typical bateau was 58 feet long and propelled by both the current and poles used to push off against the bottom of the river. Starting in 1985, replica bateaux depart from Lynch's Landing in Lynchburg for Richmond, a distance of 120 miles. (Courtesy of the *Times-Virginian*.)

Hunting season has always been eagerly anticipated in Appomattox County, and a happy hunting season used to start with a visit to Westover Paige Harvey (right) at the Kelly Woodyard. Here Harvey sells hunting licenses to Melvin Jones (left) and Leonard Drinkard (center) for $2 in the late 1960s. (Courtesy of the *Times-Virginian*.)

Campers return to their cabins after swimming at Holliday Lake in the summer of 1955. The man-made Holliday Lake was created between 1937 and 1938 as part of a work-relief measure by the Resettlement Administration and by the navy as an inland emergency landing base. The lake covers 142 acres, has two beaches, and is the site of the 4-H club camp. (Courtesy of the Virginia Department of Conservation and Recreation.)

A crowd of people cools off at Holliday Lake State Park in 1966. In 1942, the federal government leased more than 25,000 acres of the forest area to the state for 99 years. Parts of the lake area extend into Buckingham County. (Courtesy of the Virginia Department of Conservation and Recreation.)

This car is loaded with luggage and people ready to go to the 4-H camp at Holliday Lake State Park in the summer of 1942. Though the lake had been in existence less than five years, it had quickly become a local favorite in the summertime. (Courtesy of the Virginia Department of Historic Resources.)

BATTLE OF APPOMATTOX STATION

★ ★ ★
Final Blow

LEE'S RETREAT

You are standing near the site of the Appomattox Station depot on the South Side Railroad. Here, on the afternoon of April 8, 1865, Union cavalrymen under Gen. George A. Custer dealt the Army of Northern Virginia a final blow. First, they captured trains loaded with supplies for the Confederates, then they attacked and captured Gen. R. Lindsay Walker's wagons and artillery in bivouac half a mile to the north.

When word of this disaster reached Gen. Robert E. Lee at his headquarters a few miles

Gen. George A. Custer   Gen. R. Lindsay Walker

Appomattox Station in 1865 (above) – Collection of Bob Zeller
and in 1900 (below, left of bank) – Courtesy of C.P. and M.S. Sharp

northeast, he knew the end was near. He and Gen. Ulysses S. Grant had exchanged letters on the subject of surrender, and Lee had suggested a meeting between the lines the next day. With Union horsemen now blocking his escape route, Lee's only hope lay in punching through them with a combined force of infantry and cavalry, and he scheduled a breakout attack for dawn. If it failed, or if he found Federal infantry in front of him as well, then he would have no choice but to surrender.

Thousands of people each year travel General Lee's retreat route in the Virginia Civil War Trails system. Appomattox County has two waysides affiliated with the trail. This one is in Appomattox outside Appomattox Station's visitor center. (Courtesy of Virginia Civil War Trails.)

LEE'S REAR GUARD

★ ★ ★
Final Blow

LEE'S RETREAT

You are standing where Gen. James Longstreet's corps entrenched early in the morning of April 9, 1865, to protect the rear of the Army of Northern Virginia. Gen. Robert E. Lee and most of the army bivouacked about four miles south, just short of Appomattox Court House, the county seat. Here, looking south down the Confederate picket line, you can see remnants of Longstreet's earthworks, the last built in the field by the army that had become renowned for its quick and effective construction.

Gen. James Longstreet

Rear guard position of the armies on the morning of April 9. Appomattox Court House is four miles south.

New Hope Baptist Church with Confederate trenches shown at right. Painting by George L. Frankenstein.

The second retreat route sign, which explains the military situation on the morning of April 9, 1865, is located across Route 24 from New Hope Church. There is a radio program, and the sign displays both a map showing the troop positions and a George Frankenstein painting of New Hope Church as it looked in 1866. (Courtesy of Virginia Civil War Trails.)

Visit us at
arcadiapublishing.com